Clown IN The Prayer Closet

Stories From The Book Of Life

Lisa Smith-Bryant

Clown IN The Prayer Closet

Copyright © 2008 by Lisa Smith-Bryant

ISBN-13: 978-1493572809
ISBN-10: 1493572806

Acknowledgements

Father God, Lord of my life, all credit goes to you. Your word says, "Where there is no vision, the people perish: but he that keepeth the law, happy is he." Proverbs 29:18. Thank you Lord for vision and direction you keep me grounded and rooted.

To my husband Calvin Bryant, baby I love you more and more every day. You have showed me unconditional love. You have sacrificed, supported and stood by me through all of my dreams and adventures.

To my son Zon Marcell White Jr. you are a blessing. You are smart, handsome, and humble. You have grown to be an amazing man. Thanks for being my son.

Jameela Trinae Owens you have grown to be an awesome woman of God. I love you and I am so proud of you. God gave me the best daughter ever, let the Lord use you and don't look back!

Pastor Lawrence Lofton and First Lady Frances Lofton thank you for teaching me some truth. I will never forget that, "Out of the mouth of two or three witnesses every word is established."

Mother Janie Bess, the Mother of many Writers and President of WRC (Writers Resource Center) of Fairfield, you prophesied this day and here I stand.

Sharron Driver you listened to my stories for hours and hours. You are the coolest and most anointed woman I know.

Latoya Ward, you showed up and let me know that it was possible. Latoya you ushered me right into the world of the Published Author. Thank You!

For we wrestle not against flesh and blood, but against principalities, against powers, against the rulers of the darkness of this world, against spiritual wickedness in high places.

EPHESIANS 6:12

❧ *Chapter One* ❧

*T*his is the last thing I remember Pastor saying. When I opened my eyes, I was laid out in the middle of the floor. Sister Monica was praying over me, with her sweaty palms on my forehead, her hands were trembling as she blessed me in the Spirit.

"Halleluiah, halleluiah, just begin to give God the glory today, as we thank God for giving Sister Denise the baptism of the Holy Spirit," said Pastor. Sister Dana began to shout.

"Can't nobody do us like the Lord there is power in the Holy Ghost!"

This is an awesome day, today I began to speak in tongues, wait until I get home and tell my dad. He will be so proud of me.

I couldn't wait to get home, but as usual, my mom had to greet everyone who crossed her path. When we finally made it to the car, it was almost two p.m., and

1

we got out at one-twenty five p.m. All the way home my mom sang the same song over and over, "Lord make me over." This was her favorite song. Oh, did I tell you she sang it on the way there too. It's funny but all that communicating she did in church, she rarely had a conversation for me. We pulled out of the driveway; I leaped of the car so fast that I forgot to close the car door.

"Daddy, you won't believe what happened to me!"

I shouted it again, but there was no answer.

As I walked towards the den, the sound became louder and louder. Just as I walked through the door, my father jumped up and shouted.

"Touchdown!"

"Oh there you are daddy, why didn't you answer me?"

"Baby girl don't you see that the game is on, you know that on Sunday's I watch my game so whatever it is will have to wait until later."

I left my daddy alone with his game and went straight to my room, flopped down on my bed and called my potna Mona.

"What's up Mona, what y'all doin' over there?"

Mona said, "Not much I just got out of bed. I'm about to take a shower, get dressed, and go over to Red's house."

"Well Mona, I'll see you in a minute. Let me get out of these church clothes and put on something fly."

What should I wear? That Ramona is always tryin to outdo me, she know Red aint really feelin her like that. I walked over to my closet and pulled out my Dereon jeans, white silk spaghetti string shirt, my Juicy Couture purse and a pair of white sandals. I got dressed and ran downstairs, I didn't want Mona to leave me.

"Mom!"

"Mom!"

I was running down the stairs and screaming at the same time.

"Mom, can you tighten up my tracks and flat iron my hair?"

"Wait a minute Denise; I have to pick up a few things before Pastor and First Lady get here; this house is a mess. Denise, take these beer bottles outside to the recycling, empty the ashtray, oh, and spray a little air freshener."

"Man, I'm never going to get out of here. She is so self-centered. Forget the hair; I'll just put it in a pony-tail. On my worst day that chick wouldn't look better than me. Plus, I don't want to be here when Pastor and First Lady get here, enough is enough for one day."

"What was that you said Denise?"

"Nothing mom."

"Ok now little girl, don't be talking under your breath about me."

Well that's messed up, now I can't even ask for a little change.

As soon as I walked out the door, I could see my bus turn the corner. Dang I just missed it. I reached in my purse and pulled out my cell. I knew it would be another twenty minutes before the bus came. I called Mona.

"Hey Mona, I just missed the bus."

"Denise, do you want me to have Red pick you up at the bus stop?"

"Girl please, if my mom or dad walked out and saw me in the car with Red they would beat me to death."

"Well, Niece, I'll wait for you"

I guess the Lord was continuing to bless me because another bus came as soon as I got off the phone.

I got off the bus and walked a couple of blocks to Mona's house. Mona was sitting on the steps; she had on a white sun dress some gold sandals. Her hair was up in a ponytail like mine. I just love Mona my potna for real. She was truly ghetto fabulous in every sense of the way. She had on a pair of eyelashes that were so long that they touched the lenses of her glasses. Every one of her nails were airbrushed black, gold and green the color of the Jamaican flag and her toes matched. When she saw me coming she took off her glasses.

"You look hot Neice"

"You look hot yourself Mona"

"Neice, you are going to have to let me rock those shoes one day?"

"Mona, girl, you really need to stop with all the small talk, what's up with you and Red?"

"I don't know right now. We are just kickin it; you know testin out the goods."

"Umm girl, what is there to test he is fine. I aint never aint never seen no fine chocolate dude like that, plus a tight body, looks like God just carved him right out, and he's paid."

"Well Neice, if God carved him out than surely I must be the rib taken from him, so I'm just giving it back."

"Well I hope he don't lose his soul chasing that rib."

"He lost his soul a long time ago, that's why he is so paid," Mona said.

"Girl lets go, I don't want to keep my man waiting"

Just as we were walking, Red pulled up on the side of us. He was fly all the way around. He had a sixty-five Mustang with a pearl white paint job, white leather interior trimmed in gold, riding on some 22's with mustard and mayonnaise and gold knock offs. It really hurt to have to sit in the back seat while she sat up front with what really should have been my man.

Red reached over and grabbed a cigar box. Ramona opened it. It was full of weed. We rolled up to Tilden Park in Berkley Hills kicked back and smoked.

Red asked if we wanted to go to his potna's house and kick it. Ramona was down with whatever he wanted to do, and so was I. We left Tilden Park after we finished smokin and rolled over to the east, you know, east Oakland, over there on 94th and Plymouth. When we got over to his potna's house, there were about sixty motor cycles in front of the house. That really excited me. I knew we were really about to kick it. It was on and poppin, when we got out of the car. I could feel all eyes on us. I went straight into diva mode. I knew a couple of people there; I had seen them around the hood, so I was comfortable.

Red grabbed Mona's hand and she followed him while he walked around and did small talk with his boys. He acted as if Mona was going to get lost or somebody was going to snatch her up. I walked around two or three minutes before I felt a nudge on my arm. He was cute. We walked and talked for a moment, but he was a little too old for me; he said he was 22. I like them older but that's a little much.

The smoke was in the air and it made me hungrier and hungrier. I had a sudden attack of the munchies, so I made my way to the back yard. There was a long, wooden picnic table. It had a serious spread on it, ribs, chicken, links, potato salad, greens and spaghetti. I made myself a plate with a little of everything on it, not to much, got to keep the figure tight. I sat at a table at the end of the yard. I didn't want anyone to see me eating. It's hard to be a fabulous and lick sauce from your fingers.

Wouldn't you know it, Ramona and Red would walk over just when it was getting good.

"Come over here and let me introduce you to my potna, "Red said. I walked with him and Mona over to the hot tub.

"Nate here is the little cutie that I was telling you about."

Nate and Ramona took a couple of steps back like they were offering me up to a god. Nate took a couple of steps toward me not saying a word then he walked around me in a full circle. No one said a word. Nate walked over to Red and gave him a high five.

"I guess you was right man, she is thick. What's up, baby?"

Mona and Red walked away, leaving me alone with Nate. I really didn't know what to say to him. He was a little more than I expected. Twenty years old he had his own home, a fat Benz in the drive way and a Harley in the garage. I had heard a few things about him in the hood, but I never tried to get at him because he had baby mommas all over the place. Umm, there might be a couple here, but as long as they stay in check it's all good.

"My name is Denise."

"I know who you are Lil Momma, I have been peepin you for a minute now. I see you around trying to play that square roll. What it is for real?"

I didn't even get a chance to answer before he grabbed me by the waist and pulled me close to him. Nate grabbed my hand and ran his finger back and forth in the middle of palm of my hand. I started to feel strange and at ease in a strange sort of way. I stood there just staring, he was gorgeous. Nate's eyes were the color of a beautiful green emerald and they sparkled like a flawless diamond. His skin looked like he was airbrushed in caramel and it didn't have a pimple, scratch, mole or scare on it. Before I knew it his lips were on mine and I was no longer in control.

"Hey baby, you want to come out and kick it a little later after everyone leaves?"

He gave me a card with his cell number on it and just walked away, just like that. He left me alone to try to figure out just how I was going to get out of the house at nighttime.

Ramona walked over.

"What's up Denise?" Ramona said.

"Girl, it's going down, you are going to have to help me get out the house tonight because it's on."

"Anyway, girl looks at Nate and Red over there talking and cutting up… if you hook up with Nate it will be on this summer." Don't forget we only have two weeks of school left.

"Mona, why don't you ask your mom if I can spend the night over your house?" That way I can spend some time with Nate, then come over your house and from there to school."

"That will work my sista. I want to spend a little time with Red anyway and you know my mom is cool."

"Ask Red to drop me off a couple of blocks away from the house, then five minutes later call me, and ask if I can spend the night."

We had it all figured out. Mona and I walked over to Nate and Red. The closer we got to them; I could tell they were having a business conversation. It looked a little intense. I could hear part of the conversation; Nate was telling Red that he needed him to tighten things up on the streets, so that he could be free to concentrate on the car detail shop he owned over in the West. They stopped talking when we got close. Red looked at Mona and told her to go get in the car. Nate had cancelled Red's fun and put him on punishment as if he were a child sending him to his room. Red dropped me off a couple of blocks from my house as planned. I walked in the door. My mom was sitting in the living room on the computer. Before she could ask about my day, I just began to spill out all kind of lies, with the same mouth that was pouring out blessings earlier that day.

"I went over to Mona's house, and then we went to the lake and worked on our book reports."

"Wonderful Denise, I can always count on you to be responsible and get things done. You are really growing up to be such a wonderful young lady."

"Hey baby girl what was that you wanted to tell me earlier?"

"Nothing daddy, it wasn't much."

I tell you we serve a right on time God because the phone started ringing.

"Hello this is Millie Ann."

"Hey Auntie, this is Mona, and I just wanted to know if Neice could come over and help me with my math homework?"

"Didn't you two study together all day?"

"Yes Auntie, but we didn't get to the math. I thought I could do it myself, if I don't get some help I am going to get a F."

"Honey, I know what you mean. Math has never been my strongest asset; let me get Denise for you."

My mother yelled, "Denise the phone is for you!"

When she turned around I was right there and she handed me the phone.

"Hey who is this?"

"Girl you know who this is, so stop playin."

"Anyway, what you need?"

"No, umm what you need?" Mona said.

"Mona let me call you back; I will ask my mom if I can spend the night."

"Mom can I spend the night over Mona's house, I can go to school from there?"

"I don't see why not Denise."

"Thank you mom, I will ask daddy to drop me off at Mona's."

I didn't want to ask my mom to give me a ride to Mona's and risk the chance that she would come in and talk to Miss Tanya, Mona's mother. There is no telling what might come out of Miss Tanya's mouth when she opens it.

"Hey what was that you wanted to tell me earlier baby girl," daddy said?

"Daddy can you give me a ride to Mona's house?"

"Hurry up baby girl; I'm on my way to Stan's house!"

He must have won money on the game because there were no questions. The truth is my dad never paid any attention to me at all. When I was ten, I started playing sports so that I could be a part of his world. That lasted for one month, the first time I injured myself my mother said, this is no way for my future First Lady to act, so she made me a clone of herself. No wonder daddy never paid any attention to me. He barely looks in her direction.

⚛ *Chapter Two* ⚛

While daddy was driving down the street, I had all kind of crazy thoughts going through my mind. Nate had become a fixture in every thought; he had totally captured my mind. I couldn't wait to get to Mona's house so that I could call him.

When I got to Mona's house she was so excited. We were already tight, but now we had dudes that were just as tight as we are; now that's the bomb. The first thing I did was call Nate.

"What's Hattening" Nate said?

"Hey Nate"

"Who is this?"

"It's Denise I just called to see what you was doing."

"Waiting for you."

"Is that right" I said.

"Where you at?"

"Mona's"

"You want me to pick you up" Nate said?

"I'll be there in about fifteen minutes."

"Ok."

When I got off the phone Mona and I sat around and talked. Ms. Tanya, Mona's mom walked in the room. She had one of those old fashioned quilted robes and she was sportin those huge pink rollers that she never took out unless her feet were about to hit the pavement, then she looked as good as Mona and as young. She told Mona to get her an ashtray, and then she looked my way.

"You know you in the church don't be out here messin and get yourself knocked up."

I tried to listen, but Ms. Tanya kept blowing her smoke in my face. Ms. Tanya was the only grown woman I knew who smoked Black and Mild's. Mona walked in and handed her the ashtray.

Ms. Tanya looked at Mona, "You know the game, don't come here with no swollen belly, you better take care of yourself. You know if a man don't put a little change in your hand then he don't appreciate you, cause you can best believe he givin it to somebody."

If Mona wasn't so black she would have turned red. I knew she was embarrassed, but I knew how Ms. Tanya was. I was so caught-up in Tanya's craziness that I didn't hear Nate outside honking. Ms. Tanya looked outside the window and saw Nate's car.

Honey Child, you might be a tad bit out of your league with this one, never less, if you play make him pay."

He honked the horn again, I almost ran outside. It took all of my strength to keep my composure. Usually, if boy honked his horn I wouldn't even turn my head, but it was cool. I went outside and there it was black on black Benz a two seater, with the gold kit all the way around, and white leather interior trimmed in black. Nate's Benz was sitting on some shinny fat white walls.

Nate looked a little more laid back; he was wearing jeans and a white T. He got out the car and opened my door. After I sat down, he reached over me buckled my seatbelt then he kissed me. He made me feel safe and secure.

We stopped at the liquor store, he hopped out the car and ran in the store and was out just that fast. Nate handed me the bag, inside was a bottle of yack, a blunt and a box of condoms. *That's good he's into safe sex, at least I don't have to worry about being the next baby's momma.*

When we pulled up in front of his house, everything looked totally different, now that everyone was gone. He had a nice yard in front, well taken care of, but it was the inside that was on hit. The living room had white leather, brass and glass tables, phat sixty inch HD TV on the wall and under the TV was a two hundred and fifty gallon aquarium full of salt water tropical fish. They were gorgeous. Yeah, my boo has good taste.

I sat on the couch: Nate went straight to the kitchen and poured a couple of drinks. I wasn't used to drinking anything straight, but I sipped on it. We talked and laughed, he was smooth.

"Hey baby check this out, why don't we jump in the hot tub and relax a little?"

"I didn't bring a swim suite."

"It's just you and me."

I thought about it. Deep down I knew it wasn't right, and then I started to feel funny. I don't know why because I knew what was up when I left home. Before I could answer, he grabbed my hand as to say follow me, my fears were gone.

When we stopped at the hot tub, he took off his shirt. He had a well-defined six-pack and some nice arms. He had a tat on his right shoulder of praying hands: under the praying hands he had only God can judge me written in red, what would he know about that. Nate walked over to me, unbuttoned my shirt took it off and began to kiss me. I could feel him unhooking my bra. He walked behind me and began kissing my neck, and then my shirt fell to the ground. Umm he had plenty of practice. He walked back toward my front took off his clothing and stepped into the hot tub. I was left standing there with no bra or shirt on. I felt exposed and embarrassed, but the show had to go on. I tried to get sexy while he sat back and watched as I took off my pants, but I felt really cheap. The cheaper I felt the bigger my sip got and I began to feel a little better. The way he looked at me with those deep emerald green eyes let me know that it wouldn't be long before he made a move. Then I stepped into the tub.

"You know what I like about you," Nate said.

"What."

"You're different"

"How?"

"You stood out today. All those other chicks had on miniskirts, see-through shirts, and everything else they could imagine to catch a brothers eye. But you, you looked fresh, natural and well put together. You weren't all up in a brotha's face tryin to see whose pockets you could dig into. You sparkled: when you smiled I knew that I had to see what you were about."

I just looked at him. Okay I see that he is going to flatter me to death before he tries to get some.

The water felt so good. The jets were right on my back. They felt absolutely wonderful. He grabbed me and pulled me toward him. By this time, I was completely in the zone and totally relaxed. He massaged my shoulders, and kissed my neck. He made me feel so good.

"Let's go inside." He whispered in my ear.

I followed him dripping wet, no towel, no nothing, to his bedroom. I sat on side of the bed. He sat on the other side.

"You smoke?"

"Every chance I get." I said.

He rolled up a blunt and passed it to me. I hit it a couple of times and passed it back to him, he said he didn't smoke. I knew I couldn't smoke the whole thing by myself so I hit it a couple more times. I was so high that I didn't see him put on the condom, but when I turned around it was on. I laid back on his bed. He got up and put on a CD. Wow, of all things Marvin Gaye, "Let's Get It On."

It sounded good. He lay right beside me and asked me did I want some. I never answered him. I just smiled. I closed my eyes. He was so gentile. I laid there as if I were a virgin. I didn't have a lot of experience, I hoped it didn't show. I really think it turned him on he was used to being with hoochies.

He kissed me all over and I mean all over. He massaged my body with cherry flavored massage oil. Then it was on. *Oh, man I'm in love*. When he was done he wrapped his arms around me, then he laid his lips on the bottom part of my ear and whispered about how good it was. He hugged me, before I knew it we were sleep. Yeah, you right, my mind was blown.

A few hours passed. I opened my eyes the room was pitch black. I could tell that it was past midnight.

Suddenly there was an extremely loud knock at the door. Nate looked at me.

"You expecting someone lil momma?"

"No" I was too ashamed to tell him that I told Mona to pick me up so that we wouldn't be late for school. Nate got up, put on his robe and went to the door. It was Red and Mona: Nate sat in the living room and talked to Red. I guess Mona knew I was in the room because she came straight to it. We looked at each other and laughed.

"Girl, you nasty, you got to give me all the 411. First was it good?"

"If I explained it, you couldn't comprehend it. I'm still trying to put it together myself."

I got myself together then we went down to the living room, sat down and had a few drinks. Then I said, "We gotta go to school in the morning."

Red got out of his seat and Mona right behind him; this was beginning to be a pattern. That was my cue, I stood up, and Nate came over and grabbed me from behind and asked me if I was sure I couldn't stay. I told him that I had to make it to school, but I would call him.

When Mona and I got back to her house, I went straight to the shower. I couldn't wait to get in bed and marinate in my memories. Just as I laid down, before I could get my body completely on the bed, Mona began to drill me. It was funny but I really didn't want to discuss it with her. She was my best friend, but this experience was so deep and personal that I wanted to keep it to myself.

However, I did get enough strength together to let her know that he threw it on me. I knew that is what she wanted to hear, but it was much more than that. She laughed and began to tell me about her date with Red. She said that they really didn't do much. They just sat at his house while some of his boys came by, bought some dope bagged it up and left while she lay across the bed watching movies and eating Chinese food. After his boys left Mona said they messed around a little than picked me up.

"Oh yeah Neice, I forgot to tell you, I met Red's Mom." I looked at her. I knew that when a man introduces you to his mom he really likes you. Mona must have known what I was thinking.

"Girl, it aint what you think," she said. We were on our way to get the Chinese food when Red spotted his mom on San Pablo street, she looked like Skelator. She had smoked all the nutrition out of her bones, and as old as she was she had the nerve to be standing on the track tryin to catch a date. She was wearing a short black spandex dress. She needed some spandex pants under it, because the woman had track marks on every vein in her leg. She looked like she was mixed with Mexican and Black she had long jet-black hair it was beautiful. You could tell that she was something else in her day because she had managed to retain some of those qualities.

"She spotted Red and Ran to him like a stallion at Golden Gate Fields. The first thing she asked him was if he had anything for her. He handed her a fifty-dollar bill. Red tried to hold a conversation with her but after she got that change in her hands, she couldn't talk any more. She started shaking and talking really fast, so Red just pulled off."

Mona said she grabbed his hand and told him not to trip, but Nate just felt the need to start explaining. I just listened as he talked about his mother being a dope fiend while she was pregnant with him. Straight from the hospital Red went to go live with his granny. His granny had legal custody of him until he was twelve, then she passed away. He was forced to go back to his mother's house where he has been getting his money and putting food on the table not only for himself, but for his little brother and sister. He said, "Thank God my granny prayed for me, so I'm all good, because she was faithful. Mona said a whole different look came over him when he began to speak of his granny. Mona didn't understand, but I did. I understood why Red gave Mona everything she wanted. He was use to being a provider. It was second nature for him to help those he chose to help, and at the same time to destroy

those he chose to destroy. I knew enough about Red to
know that he might be sensitive about his family, but
he wasn't no joke on those streets and no one I knew
would think about giving him any problems about
anything. That's why Nate chose him as his right hand.
Red was a soldier no doubt. I guess if she is cool with
that then I am too. Oh man I forgot to pray, let me get
out of bed.

Father God in the name of Jesus,

Forgive me of my sins,

Wash me in your blood,

Give me peace in the midst of tragedy,

Love me the way that only you can,

Thank you for the gift, in the name of Jesus.

The next day at school I was so tired I could barely
function. I dozed off in second period three or four
times. *God give me strength, I feel completely drained.*
Ramona and I had third period together. She looked
fine; I guess she was use to it. She helped me stay awake
in class, but it was a struggle. Finally, I had to call my
mom at work and ask if I could come home. I told her
I was sick to my stomach. Mom called the attendance
office and they gave me a permission slip to go home.
Lucky me, the bus came right away. I didn't have to
stand in the hot sun for long, it was only eleven–thirty
am, and the temperature was eighty two degrees, Lord
have mercy.

I was awakened by a voice.

"Where are you going honey?" the bus driver asked me.

I had missed my stop. I had to ride the bus all the way back around which is a forty-five minute ride.

∽ *Chapter Three* ∽

My daddy was a big man. He was 6 feet 3 inches tall and about 270 pounds, and a little chunky around the middle section, but he wasn't flabby he was solid. The only resemblance we shared was in our smile. I wish he would have handed down the dimples, but anyway.

He used to love to go to church. He never missed a Sunday, but when Grandma passed away and he found out that she had signed her house over to the church, a church that wouldn't even contribute to her burial expenses, he was so upset, he never went back. He says he's part of the body, he knows the Word, can recite scripture and reads the Word on a regular basis, but that's it nothing else.

My mom on the other hand is something else. She has earned herself a title, "Evangelist Millie Ann." She goes to church almost every day. Tuesdays- choir rehearsal, Wednesday- leadership, meeting Thursday-bible study, Friday- Holy Ghost Service, all this is just preparation for the big day Sunday. Pastor calls Sunday, "The Great Assembly," and it last all day. Our Pastor is a little long winded. My mom has been at the same church for 21 years. Everyone in the church community knows her. She is often asked to speak at other churches, especially during revivals. My mother can sing. When my mother stands up, even before she can get a note out people just start shoutin, because they know what's about to come.

I spend a lot of time in church with my mom. If I have a lot of homework she might let me stay home, but most of the time she makes me bring it to church. I've been in the church so long that at sixteen years old, I believe that I could run a ministry all by myself. Since I started high school my grades have been good. That's the reason they allow me to have a little free-dom. I caught on to that concept in middle school. One semester I got two D's on my report card, needless to say all my after school activities were cancelled until the next report card. All I needed to say was that I needed to go to the library or do a project with a friend and they would let me go. I was also smart enough to know that I had better have a paper trail to follow it up. I try really hard to keep a 3.5 or 4.0 GPA and I even had a 4.5 twice. The only chores I have are my bedroom and my bathroom.

Every once in a while my mother might ask me to vacuum, load the dishwasher, or something. Their main focus was school. I really didn't date. The only boys they allowed me to go out with were boys whose parents had positions in the church. I was a rookie compared to some of them, plus I didn't want my business in the street like that, you know how some people gossip. You know, like when my mom and her church friends get on the phone, they gossip so much that they forget they are all one in Christ Jesus; oh this only happens after they pray for the person first. My mom also has a prayer partner, sounds like gossip to me, but it's their story, they can tell it any way they want to.

So far, I have been all that my parents expect me to be. I dress well, I communicate well, I know the word and look good on paper. In their eyesight I could do no wrong. I know one thing. If I am going to continue to see Nate I had better keep it up. The sad thing about the whole situation is that things were already going downhill. You see, up until eleven-thirty today I had perfect attendance, but one day won't kill me. Let me get a little more rest. My mom should be home in a minute, let me call Nate before she gets home.

"Hey Nate what you got going on?"

"Nothing much what you got going on lil mama?"

"I left school early I was so tired that I couldn't concentrate."

"How come you didn't call me, I would have picked you up then you could have kicked back over here."

"I'm cool; I just need to lay my head down." I laid my head down and it was a rap. I slept harder than I had ever, and boy was it good. I woke up and my mom was already home. I didn't even hear her come in.

She was in the kitchen cooking. My mom always tried to have dinner ready when daddy got home. I went downstairs.

"Hey Denise, how are you feeling baby?" she asked.

"I'm ok; I think I was sick from something I ate this morning."

"Good, you can help me get started. Maybe I'll go take a shower, I feel really sweaty."

"Go ahead, I'll cook." I was happy when it was almost done. It was almost ninety-five degrees at five –thirty pm.

My daddy walked in the door.

"Smells good in here baby girl where's your momma?"

"She went upstairs to take a shower."

"How was school today?"

"It was ok. I didn't stay all day because I didn't feel well, but I'm ok now."

"Well, I'm happy you're ok baby girl. Could you get me a cold one out of the fridge?"

It never fails, when my daddy gets home from work the first thing he does is sit down, drink a beer and as he calls it collect his thoughts. This took somewhere between thirty minute to an hour and a half and at least three beers. Collecting his thoughts meant that he had a little buzz going. I had it figured out.

My mom came back downstairs; she had changed into her silk pajamas and slippers. Everyone says I look just like her. She is 40 years old but you couldn't tell it, not with that video chick body. It defiantly wasn't the body of a woman who had given birth to three children; two in college. My two brothers are 22 and 19 years old. My younger brother followed my oldest brother off to college. Yeah, my momma was something else in her day. That's how she snagged my daddy.

She doesn't know it, but I know she was pregnant with my oldest brother before they got married. My grandma on my daddy's side made it her business to tell me one day when she was mad at my mom. That's why she left her house to the church, she couldn't imagine my mom ever living in it. She could have left it to me or my brothers, but that's what hate will do.

Dinners ready, I had finished it. We had fried chicken baked potatoes and salad. After I finished eating I excused myself from the table and went upstairs. I could hear my parents talking; money was tight with both of my brothers in college. My father made thirty-five an hour as a journey man heavy equipment operator. He had been on the job for twenty years. My mom was the church secretary. Our church was huge almost three thousand members; we had three services on

Sunday. This was a full time job for her and she took it seriously. What she couldn't finish at work she bought home with her. The money was good she was on salary $3500 a month.

This still wasn't enough, my parents struggled to pay bills and at times that caused a serious strain in their marriage. Today was one of those days. I sat at the top of the stairs and listened.

"Millie Ann, I think we need to cut down on some of our expenses. Every time I look around more money is going out, without more money coming in.

"Are you complaining about being a dad?"

"Are you complaining about the boys getting an education?"

"Are you complaining about the house note?"

"Oh, maybe you are just tire of being married."

"Ok I get it; you just can't stand to be blessed, you just need Jesus!"

My dad never got a word in. I didn't know at that point if my mom was loading up the dish washer or just breaking the dishes.

Ramona called me. She said she was about to come over and spend the night because her mom's boyfriend was over. She didn't like the way he looked at her, she knew what's up, so she stayed out of his way when he came. She wanted to tell her mother but she couldn't. He treated her really well, he even paid bills around the house, which left Mona's mom a little money to give Mona so she could have lunch money and basic necessities. Red provided the rest. Mona had learned early to depend on men the same way her mother had.

Mona was more than my best friend. She was my soul mate, my confidante someone who I could go to when there was no one else. I knew she felt the same about me.

Mona knocked at the door. I answered it. My parents continued to argue, as if no one had walked in the house. I looked at the both of them, I wondered if they would have done that if Pastor and First lady had walked in.

Every year our church sponsors teen evangelism conferences. Our church is the largest church in Oakland so we sponsor it, and other churches visit. This was really going to mess up my schedule. I already knew my mother signed me up for every event, they had going. She always did stuff like that. It didn't matter if I wanted to do it or not. I think she was trying to groom me for church leadership. I asked Mona if she was participating this year, she said no. I knew her relationship with Red had something to do with it. I'm surprised she didn't spend the night over there. They follow each other like night and day. When night comes, you know day is around the corner.

We sat up and talked a while mostly about Nate and Red making plans for the summer. Finally, we fell asleep. The morning came really fast, but I sure felt a lot better than I did the day before. Mona called Red and asked him if he would pick us up and give us a ride to school.

It was all good, my dad left around 7:30am and my mom was right behind him. Red was on time. We shot to the car like bullets. I hoped none of my neighbors would tell my mom or dad. Mona was really feeling Red. She had gone past the stage of testing the goods. I could see her evolving into a new person bit by bit. She even started dressing different. Even in the hottest weather Mona didn't wear those low cut jeans and little t-shirts. Don't get me wrong, there's nothing wrong with it, but it wasn't her style. She usually dressed in a nice pair of jeans with the matching shoes and a purse or in weather like this cute summer dress, that's how we got down. I guess we all slum once in a while, including myself.

We pulled in front of the school, Red kissed Mona and told her he would be out of town a couple days because he had to make a run for Nate, but he would be back by Friday. Then he handed her a hundred dollars, she got out of the car and I was right behind her. As soon as I got out of Red's car my cell phone rang, it was Nate. He wanted to pick me up at lunch and take me out to eat, it was all good. I told Mona, she asked if she could go. I told her if it was cool with Nate, I didn't care. First, second and third period just seemed to go on forever.

When the bell rang Mona and I walked to the front of the school. Nate was right there. I asked if Mona could come with us, he said no, he just wanted to spend time with me. You should have seen the look on Mona's face. I could tell she was a little shocked. It was funny because whoever she dated I usually went out with them and vice versa so this threw her off a little, but I was really excited about being alone with him. I looked at Mona and told her I would bring her back something. She said okay and walked away.

I asked Nate where we were going to eat. He said it was a surprise, so I kicked back and enjoyed the ride. Before I knew it we were going over the Bay Bridge. I looked at Nate, at this point I was panicked. I was going to be late going back to school. I told Nate I had to go back, I had never cut class, it would ruin my record plus my parents would find out. He looked at me and said, "You need to relax, little momma, one time won't hurt, if you have been that faithful you have earned it."

You know I have, plus I wouldn't get to see him later because tonight I would have to go to church with my mom. It felt so good to be with Nate. He had a way of making me feel so comfortable, special and safe.

On the way he stopped by the flower shop and came out with the most beautiful rose, a rich burgundy. It looked as if he had poured a deep red wine on it and sprinkled his love on it. After he handed it to me he kissed me and told me the beauty of the rose didn't even compare to mine. Wow, this was deep. I tried so hard to make myself believe that what was going on was okay, but deep down it didn't feel okay.

The restaurant had lavender table cloths, a flowered centerpiece on each table with lavender mixed in each centerpiece, which filled the air with a rich and warm aroma. I had never been to an Italian restaurant before. It was so nice.

The menu didn't have any prices on it. I was too embarrassed to ask Nate if we had some kind of spending limit. I ordered manicotti and salad. Nate had a seafood platter.

We talked and talked mostly about my family and myself. Nate didn't really like to talk about himself he acted as if he was part of the CIA or something. When we left the restaurant we went over to the ice cream parlor for some frozen yogurt.

Mona called me and asked me where I was, school was out. Oh my God! I had totally lost track of time, it was 3pm. I told Nate I had to be home by 4pm.

We walked so fast, we were jogging as we made our way to the car. The freeway entrance was close by. We were in a really big hurry.

Nate smashed once we were on the freeway. We were over the bridge in no time and I was home by 4:15pm. I lucked out, I have plenty of time to spare before mom gets home... or so I thought.

Busted, busted, and busted again. As soon as I walked into the house, my dad was right there on the phone. I tried to be cool but, by the look on his face I knew things went terribly wrong. "Where the hell have you been?"

He told the person on the phone he would call back when my mom got home. I didn't know what to say, plus he didn't give me time to answer. He was all up in my face; I knew if I had said something wrong he was going to knock me out. I didn't even know what he knew, so I didn't want to say the wrong thing but I had to say something. So, I asked him, what he was talking about. I should have never done that.

"Do you think I'm some kind of fool?" He said.

"No daddy."

"Then where the hell have you been since lunch? Your school called, your science teacher said she saw you earlier today, but you never showed up for class. So did your Spanish teacher and they checked the office, no one gave you permission to leave."

"I went out to lunch with my friend and his car broke down."

"What friend Denise?" Now I knew he was really mad he never called me Denise. "Give me your cell phone!"

I reached in my purse and handed it to him. As I was handing daddy my cell, it rang. I was praying he wouldn't answer it, but he did. It was Nate. My heart was beating so hard I thought I would die right there on the spot. He asked Nate were we together today and he said yes. Oh, my God! I felt a slight stroke coming over my body. My dad told Nate to come over around 6pm because he wanted to meet him.

It was all bad. He was waiting for my mom to get home, plus this was choir rehearsal night, if she had to miss it for something crazy, my ass was really out. Daddy told me to go to my room and we would deal with it when my mom got home.

All the time I was in my room, I prayed.

"Father God in the mighty name of Jesus, I am so sorry please show up and help me through this, I will never do this again, amen."

I even anointed myself, but I got no peace because I knew my mom was going to kill me. I was so in tune with my surroundings that I heard the door open downstairs with my bedroom door closed. I could hear my parents talking, my mom getting louder and louder.

"Denise! Get down stairs now and tell me what's going on."

One thing I could say about my parents, they might be saved, but they aint no fools. They got a little game when it comes to them streets especially daddy, he definitely aint no fool. I had no choice. I told them I met Nate over the weekend and he asked me out to lunch. Time just got away from us. Before I could get another word out the bell rang.

My dad answered the door. It was Nate. He didn't even look nervous. I don't know how he could be so cool, because I was heated. The first thing my father asked Nate is if he knew how old I was. He said "Yes, she's 16 going on 17 next month." Then my mom jumped in and asked how old he was, he said that he just turned 20 last month. My dad's eyes bulged out so far I thought he was going to blow his cool. He asked him what the hell he wanted with me. Nate said that he enjoyed my company. My dad made it very clear that he would not be enjoying my company anymore and that if he even tried to see me again he would break his ass off. My mother just looked at me and shook her head. I knew I had messed up.

Nate left and my mom told me to go upstairs to my room. When I didn't get a whooping, I knew things were really bad. Now my dad was getting louder and louder and my mom was cool.

I got up at the regular time, one thing was different. My mom was still home.

"Denise you don't have school today" she said when she walked into my room. "Your dad and I decided you can do home studies since there are only two weeks left. Today I am going to see your counselor to arrange everything."

That was the most depressing moment of my life. All I could do was cry, my life was over.

My mom told me to sit down so that she could talk to me. I will never forget the look on her face, it wasn't anything but pure disappointment.

"Baby let me tell you something, you know your friend Nate?"

"Yeah, momma."

"Well I know him, too. He's every mom's worst nightmare, you know that girl on crack, or that girl on the corner, or that teenager about to give birth well they all had a Nate in one way or another, thank God for his favor. Thank God that this thing didn't go too far."

My mom looked at me and said baby, if you never know anything else know this, "There is nothing new under the sun and nothing that can't be revealed because of the Son."

After she said it she got up and walked out the room. I knew that she knew. I knew that she knew about the sex, weed and my feelings for Nate. I could just tell.

It was about 10 am when my counselor finally called back and told us we could come in at 11:15am. I was kind of relieved. I hope I would see Mona and get a chance to talk to her so I could give Nate a message for me.

My mother never came to school, so people were looking at me really crazy. My counselor was cool, so I just knew that everything was going to go smooth.

Mrs. Brown asked my mom why she wanted to take me out and home school so late in the year. One thing about my mom she is definitely to the point. She came straight out and told Mrs. Brown I had become involved with an older man who she suspected was a drug dealer and she was afraid for me.

Mrs. Brown just looked at my mom. I knew she didn't believe what she was hearing. Mrs. Brown boasted about me to the other teachers. She got out of her chair and walked over and hugged me. She looked me straight in the eyes and told me that I was highly favored by God and Satan is a lie. Mrs. Brown is a member of my church and also a witness of the gift I received just a couple of days ago.

She told my mom whatever she needed that she would make it happen the best that she could. My mom said she needed all my assignments and that she would bring me to school for finals. Mrs. Brown thought this was an excellent idea. She told my mom she would have my teachers e-mail my assignments, then my mom could fax them back to the school three times a week and she would make sure my teachers received them.

We left the school and went straight to my mom's job. One thing was for sure. My mom definitely wouldn't tell anybody in the church. My mother told me I could go to work with her every day. I knew my life was over, I couldn't talk on the phone, go outside, watch

TV, listen to the radio or go to school. I felt like I was in hell. I just sat in the bathroom at my mom's job and cried, that was all I could do. I finally realized just how bad my situation was.

My dad will probably never look at me the same. How can I be baby girl when I was living a grown woman's life? My mother lost all her faith in me; she no longer felt she could leave me unsupervised. I couldn't talk to Mona because I was being punished and if I saw Nate again my day would kill us both.

School which was my greatest accomplishment, had been snatched right away from me as if I had no say. And now my teachers who had trusted me to grade papers, take attendance and occasionally work in the office would never see me the same way again. How could I make such a mess of life in three days?

God I am so embarrassed and ashamed. I didn't even know I had those things and feelings inside me. Please show me your grace and mercy. I repent of those things. I am so sorry.

I didn't know I was speaking out loud and I didn't know that anyone else was in the bathroom. It was First Lady.

"Who is that in there," she said? She knocked on the stall.

"It's me, Denise."

"Come out of there and let me see you. What's wrong with you honey?"

"I really messed up." I began to tell her about Nate and how I messed up in school, my parents didn't trust me anymore and I had sinned against God. The worst part was that I still loved Nate and that I couldn't get him out of mind no matter what happened, he was still there.

She said she was going to talk to Pastor about counseling for me. I asked her not to tell my mother, I was really taking a leap of faith, but she said okay. She hugged me and told me that no matter what, she loved me, and that we all go through things. She told me to wash my face and get myself together. She told me, I was a child of the God most high. First lady said because Jesus was raised from the dead he overcame death and if I was serious about my repentance I could also overcome death. I hugged her and told her thank you. I had a little peace now but I still had to make things right with my parents, who trusted me and counted on me to be able to do the right thing. First lady walked out the door and said, "Baby, sin no more."

I left the bathroom and went to my mom's office. The only thing I could do was look at her and tell her how sorry I was. I broke down and began to cry all over again. This time I couldn't pull myself together I was completely overcome. It was as if my tears were a way of removing the sin, the more I cried the lighter my spirit felt.

My mother came over and pulled me closer to her, the way she used to do when I was little, when I fell off my bike or skates. This time I just fell in a different way. She kissed my forehead and said, "I know." She pulled a chair next to her desk and began to tell me a story. This was unusual because my mom never talked about her childhood. All I knew was that her dad was a Pastor, her mom was a Minister and that two of my uncles were Pastors, one of them a Bishop in the Church Of God In Christ, and my aunt Evelyn was a Missionary.

She began to tell me about this boy she used to date named Steven when she was about 16. Steven's family had a lot of money and they paid tithes in the church so her parents allowed her to date him. They never looked at who he was as a person. Mom said she fell in love with Steven and ended up pregnant. Steven was her first. When she told Steven she was pregnant, he said the baby wasn't his. In those day they didn't have all the the privacy for girls that they have now, so she had to tell her parents. Her parents put her out that's how she ended up in California. In her fifth month she had a miscarriage. My grandma's church on my daddy's side took her in.

"So, Denise. I know Nate." She said. "Everybody has a Nate. Nate is that obstacle that keeps you from being all you can be. Thank God for Jesus, because those

Nate's are powerless against him. Denise, don't ever think you can't come to talk to me because I have been there, and so has everyone else, I don't care about how perfect they seem to be."

I felt much better now I knew my life was back on track. Even if I didn't have any privileges, it didn't matter as long as my mom didn't hate me.

The Pastor had called a staff meeting, so I asked my mom if I could get on the computer for a while. These meetings usually lasted an hour. I logged on to Facebook. Nate had been trying to contact me. I went I went to his page and we started messaging each other. Thank God he was on. He told me he was thinking about me but he couldn't afford any problems. He didn't even ask me how things were going or if I got in trouble, but he did tell me he couldn't see me any-more, even though he enjoyed kicking it with me and I was cool. He said he was at the detail shop and had to go and take care of business.

Now I knew my place, I was nothing more to him than a good time. Yeah, he liked me but he also like those baby mamas at one time. I felt really betrayed and used. I had given the best part of myself and then was just tossed aside like a snot rag.

I felt so bad but regardless of the situation I loved God. I had let him down, and it was making me sick. How come I didn't see him for what he really was? The

Holy Spirit had been ministering to me the whole time. That is what those feelings were each time I was about to do the wrong thing. Too bad I didn't listen.

I logged on to Mona's Facebook even though I knew she wasn't home from school yet. I wanted to let her know that I would be logged on tomorrow at 2a.m. that way I knew my parents would be asleep and that I could catch up on a few things.

Let me be honest, I really wanted to know about Nate. The truth is, I would have crept over there given the opportunity. I could hear my mom's footsteps getting closer, so I went to another website. Thank God for high speed internet, it's a wonderful thing.

I was so busy being sneaky, I didn't notice the look on her face. She looked me directly in the face.

"Why did you tell my business? Don't you have any respect for anything or anyone?"

It dawned on me there was no staff meeting. They were meeting about me. I was scared to go home. Mom couldn't let loose in the church, home was totally different. This hour is going to go really fast. All I could hear over and over was a voice in my head saying dead girl walking. That voice was soon drowned out.

"Denise, get your things together, we're about to leave."

Chapter Four

There was no music, there was no arguing, not even a slap across the face, there was nothing. How do you respond to nothing? On my way home? I was afraid to say anything because it could very well set her off. I looked down and noticed my mom had ruined her stockings. Now I knew she was heated because, it was nothing for my mom to take off her stockings rub on some lotion and put her heels back on before you could blink. Imperfection was not an option, even while driving home from work.

Maybe I could catch a break, tonight is her leadership meeting. Momma was usually so filled with the spirit after the church elders met that nothing bothered her, even household problems would be put on hold. I had a plan, I was going to go straight upstairs, take a shower, put on my gown and fall asleep. The heck with dinner. Maybe silence is wonderful and I ought to take advantage of it. You really don't know, once my mom opened her mouth it was going to be total devastation, worse than any hurricane could ever imagine.

About a half a mile from the house I began to feel sick. My mouth was watering like a faucet. I couldn't turn it off. I had to ask her to pull over.

Silence was broken at this point. When she pulled over I began to vomit all over the place. I didn't have time to put my head outside. It just started gushing out everywhere and boy was it foul. Momma held her hands up and just began to surrender.

"Father, please don't let her be pregnant in the name of Jesus." She was crying so hard I didn't think she would be able to drive. Each time a car pulled up on the side of us they just stared, please don't let me see anyone I know.

We finally made it home. That was the roughest ride that I had ever taken. The car door opened. This time mom was out of the car and inside the house. She went straight upstairs, took a shower and went straight to bed. The script had been flipped on me. No dinner, leadership meeting, what would daddy think when he got home and found out the events of the day. What would his response be?

I went upstairs to wash that foul smell off me. Right in the middle of my shower it dawned on me, mom thought I was pregnant. How was I going to fix this before my dad got home? There was only one logical thing to do, call Isaiah. My brother Isaiah was cool. I could talk to him then he could talk to mom before dad got home.

On the other hand if I told one more person, even my brother it could get a whole lot worse than it is. The phone rang. It was Auntie Munch, my mom's younger sister. Auntie Munch was thirty-two years old, she lived in Virginia. When she was a baby she would eat everything in sight, and she still loved to eat, this is how she earned her name. I had only met her twice. Auntie Munch was the complete opposite of momma in personality but of course she was no doubt beautiful. Beauty ran rapid on my mom's side of the family. It was one of the many gifts God blessed them with. Auntie Munchie was the most low maintenance kicked-back person I had ever met on my mom's side. We would watch TV while she twisted her dreads. She didn't wear makeup she would say no need, if you got it flaunt it. She knew she was wonderfully and divinely made.

"Hey, Denise, you have been on my mind. How is life treating you sweetie?"

I didn't know what to say. Was this a blessing or one more thing to get me roped up? Things just couldn't get any worse than they had, or so I thought. I began to tell her what was going on; it took me at least 30 minutes.

She didn't interrupt me, not once. When I was finished she asked me if I wanted to visit her in Virginia, during summer vacation.

"You know I'm on punishment."

"You let me take care of that." Auntie Munchie said.

She told me she had bought a house on Virginia Beach and I was just the person to help her break it in. Then she said put your momma on the phone. I walked upstairs and knocked on the door.

"Momma, Auntie Munchie is on the phone." I ran downstairs and listened on the other line.

"Millie, I called because God put Denise on my heart" Auntie Munchie said. I just finished talking to her, so no need to put on a show for me. Millie Ann you of all people know what's out there in the world so pull yourself together, all that word you got inside you and when Satan attacks you up under some cover. Have you gone completely mad? I'll tell you what. Let Denise come to Virginia for a couple of weeks while you recoup, cause I know that husband of yours aint helping the situation any."

"Denise said she aint pregnant either, so calm you nerves and allow her to have a storm, we all have them. Kenneth had one yesterday and he's only three, but while he was laying there screaming and crying in the store cause he couldn't have any gum, I just walked away, right out the store. You best believe he came running behind me, got in the car and acted like he had some good sense. You discuss it with your husband, and call me tomorrow, kiss Denise for me.

Auntie hung up the phone before my mom could say anything. My auntie knew how to handle herself and she wasn't into conflict. She knew how to be cool with everyone. Auntie Munch even knew how to deal with daddy. When she was here she always bought daddy home some beer and did small talk with him. This was her way of smoothing the tension and letting him know that he could be who he wanted to be around her. The last time she was here she gave my daddy two tickets to the Raiders game worth $150 a piece, but she didn't have to buy them. You see the favor of God followed my Auntie wherever she was. People loved to give her things, but what you have to know is that she was a natural giver herself.

I sat on the couch and watched my mom as she walked down the stairs. There was something different, she was looking rough. Mom usually looked as good at night as she did in the day.

Daddy walked in the door he looked worn out. He didn't even grab a beer and relax his nerves. He had found another way and another place to make things better for himself. You know now that I look back on things, I see this is the way they always handled problems. Ignore them and maybe they will go away.

I grabbed a bucket of Pine Sol so that I could clean mom's car. I could smell the car as I approached it. Sin stinks, I thought to myself. I scrubbed until my knuckles were raw. I didn't want there to be any signs left of this day. Maybe today is better forgotten, I thought to myself. After all tomorrow is a new day.

My dad left his cell on the table and the temptation became great. Before I knew it the phone was in my hand and I was talking to Mona.

"What's up, girl? Where you at?"

Ramona said that she was out with Red. He was back from his trip and he wanted to kick it. While we were talking I heard Nate's voice in the background

"How come Nate is out to dinner with you and Red?"

"Necie, while I was waiting for Red to pick me up from school today I saw September and we started talking, anyway Red and Nate pulled up. Nate got out the car and started talking to her, so we're all here together just nibbling on a few wings." In the background I heard Nate say, "you don't owe that girl no explanation about what I do, hang up the phone."

I knew Mona had set Nate up with September. That's all right she aint nothing but a tramp anyway, the four of them deserved each other. I was hecka mad, betrayed and humiliated by my best friend, so she could stay in good with a low life. I thought we was tighter than that, but I guess she never promised anything either.

My head was pounding I definitely could not sleep. I really needed to go to bed so this day could be over as soon as possible, but I needed answers. About 1 a.m. I decided to call Mona back, I didn't even give her a chance to say hello before I let her have it.

"How come you set September up with Nate, you was foul for that one."

"What you want me to do, Denise? I aint on punishment, don't be mad at me because you shut down. What am I supposed to do? Did you really expect for me to tell Nate he couldn't talk to September, come on now."

I hung up the phone. I felt stupid all over again. Mom had just spoken to me about standing alone before God, and that I did. I stood there in his holy presence, everyone in the house was asleep and the Holy Spirit had met me in my room. I began to feel embarrassed. God began to flash my life before my eyes and the choices I had made. He even went as deep as to show me each time he had sent his spirit down to give me an escape. Sweat began to run from my forehead into my eyes, blinding me and forcing me to close my eyes to the natural and enter into the spirit.

The power of the Holy Ghost rained on me and I began to pray in my holy language. Yes, I was speaking in tongues again. I didn't know what I was saying but my spirit was having a serious conversation with God. The best part is that he had shown up right in the middle of my room as I sat on the edge of my bed.

God spoke some things into my spirit about relation-
ships. God sowed me how he had given marriage as
a gift to Adam and Eve, they were created especially
for each other. Marriage and sex wasn't created just
for pleasure, culture or convenience. God showed me
that marriage was a symbol of the church which is
us and the kingdom instituted by God. When man
leaves his parents and in a public act he promises himself to his wife, it's the same way we leave the world,
and before witnesses we accept Jesus as our Lord and
Savior. The husband and wife agree to be there for each
other above all others, the same way we agree to be
servants of God and to follow, be obedient and worship
Jesus, seeking him first above all others. Then as a gift
he gave sex to seal the covenant when their bodies are
locked together as one. It symbolizes one person, one
flesh, and one spirit.

This is why I couldn't shake Nate. I had entered into
a covenant with him and joined in spirit. The problem
is that it wasn't the Holy Spirit because we were not
married and totally out of order. I now had a complete
understanding. The Spirit of Truth was on me and it
hurt, but because it was the truth it was good and holy,
it defiantly set me free.

Wisdom is wonderful.

"Thank you, Father God, for your wisdom you have
touched me in a special way, shown me your grace and
mercy, for that I thank you in the name of Jesus, amen."

I fell asleep right after that, and the presence of the Lord was on me. That peace lasted until 7a.m. I woke up blessing the day; it's a new day I said out loud! Yeah the day was new for me and the peace of the Lord was on me but it had not touched the rest of my household.

⌒ *Chapter Five* ⌒

y mom and dad were in the kitchen arguing. I threw on my robe and rushed down the stairs. I hoped my presence would stop them from acting ugly toward each together. As you may have noticed by now, my stuff dont work, this was one of them.

My very presence fueled my dad to say the most awful things to my mom. He read her history right in front of me. He didn't leave out any details, believe me when I say he dotted every I and crossed every T. Daddy used every ugly word possible to dethrone my mom and make her think she was not who she knew she was in the kingdom.

Then to top it off, he looked at me and said, "Baby girl I am so sorry you went through what you did, your momma should have schooled you a little better, she definitely has had enough experience with men."

He grabbed his coat and walked out the door. I felt so sorry for my mom; she had been humiliated right in front of me. I guess we were staying home today because mom went back to bed; she wasn't concerned about school or anything else. Quite frankly I think she was too embarrassed to be in my company.

I really wanted to hold her and let her know that everything was going to be alright and I loved her. I wanted to tell her about God's mercy and grace, but I couldn't because I had already messed up my testimony, so what could I really say. I took a bath got dressed and started my school work.

The phone rang it was my Pastor. Pastor asked me if he could speak to my mom. I told him she couldn't come to the phone because she was sick. He told me to tell her that he called, and I said ok its funny how fast you can get yourself into bondage. After all, I couldn't tell him my mom was at the middle of having a nervous breakdown. The fact of the matter is that what she really needed was wise counsel.

Three days passed before my mom came out of her room for more than ten minutes. Yesterday she came downstairs and asked me if things were going ok, I said yes and that was the extent of our conversation.

Meanwhile my life had been put on the back burner. Mom had stopped asking me about my school work; as a matter of fact she didn't monitor me at all, unless she could see through the bedroom walls.

The doorbell rang at 10a.m. I looked through the window and saw First Lady and Mother Taylor. I opened the door and they stepped right on in.

"Where is your momma, honey, I came to see how she's doing." Mother Taylor said. I asked her if I could get them anything to drink before I went upstairs to get mom out of her room.

When Mother Taylor showed up she meant business. She was there to lay hands and pray any demonic force or spirit that was in you right back into the pits of hell. Mother had practice. She had, been in the church when it was formed. There was power in those old wrinkled hands that had age spots that were older than my mother and I put together. Her husband, Bishop Taylor, had ordained the pastor that formed the church that we now reside in. Every time there was a birth in the church she would show up in the hospital and put a blessing on that baby. My father was one of those babies.

People used to say that Mother Taylor could look at you and see your spirit. Now she had come to examine mom.

As soon as mom started walking down the stairs Mother Taylor started praying and asking God for deliverance for my mom, then she rolled right into her Holy language and it was on. I don't know what she saw but she couldn't get that oil out of her purse fast enough. Mother Taylor laid her hands right on mom's forehead, then she told mom to throw her hands up as a sign of victory.

"Just begin to thank him and praise him hallelujah." Mom did just that. Meanwhile First Lady prayed over the house and blessed it touching any and everything in sight, including windows and doorways. All of a sudden Mother Taylor shouted come out of here you spirit of depression and victimization in the name of Jesus! After that they hugged mom. First Lady said, "see you tomorrow sis, your desk is backed up Pastor depends on you, you're a blessing to us all."

Mom shook her head. She was still in the spirit and unable to speak. They had come to clean house, and that they did. Mom was totally incapacitated, so I walked them to the door. Mother Taylor gave me a kiss and First Lady said take care of your mother, we will see you tomorrow.

After they left mom went from lying on the couch, to praying on her knees to finally just laying on her face flat down on the floor. Even though First Lady had asked me to watch over my mom I knew she needed her space. She had entered into her prayer closet and there wasn't room for two. I went upstairs and decided to watch a little television while my mom got herself together. Thirty minutes later I came downstairs to check on my mom. She was sitting on the couch, she patted the cushion next to her, gesturing that she wanted me to sit next to her.

"Come on baby, everything is going to be alright." I laid my head on her shoulder, and we cried together. "Sometimes you have to fight for what you love." I didn't quite understand it at the time where she was coming from, but by the end of the day it was quite clear.

∞ *Chapter Six* ∞

Millie Ann was back. Her spirit had been renewed and she was ready to fight. It had been over a week since I heard her sing but today she sang.

She wasn't only praising God but she had slipped right into worship, mom had been resurrected.

"Get dressed, baby, we have a few errands to run." Mom said. The first thing we did was stop and have a couple of banana splits; we sat and talked for about an hour. I felt like I was meeting a new friend. Mom pulled out her cell phone and called Pastor.

"I will be in tomorrow Pastor, see you soon." She flipped the cover back on her phone and we continued talking. We made two more other stops, the first was Safeway; we ran in and picked up three T-bone steaks, a bag of potatoes, and salad in the bag. This was my dad's favorite meal. The next stop was Neldoms Bakery; they made the best strawberry cakes on the face of the earth. I hated to get back in the car to head home. We were having a great time together, and boy was it a long time coming.

When we pulled in front of our driveway, mom put the car in park, sat there for a minute then she said. "Lord no more!" she stepped out of the car and began to walk around the house picking up old newspapers and pieces of trash that had blown on our lawn, then again she declared it, this time with even more authority than the first time. "Lord no more!!!"

Mom walked to the front door and started to look at the conditions of not only the outside but the inside of our living situation; things had really fallen apart while mom was down. The house was really dusty; you could see Mother Taylor fingerprints everywhere. Mom went to the laundry room to bring out the cleaning supplies, I grabbed the pledge and dust cloth, the fight was on and these were my weapons of choice. Round one was over. I cleaned the living room, dining room, and kitchen. Mom cleaned the downstairs bathroom, the guest room and bath where dad had been sleeping and vacuumed the house.

Round two, mom said let's get dressed, so we could get dinner started. Mom ran to her bathroom, and I ran to mine. I was dressed in an hour. It took my mom one hour and forty-eight minutes to get dressed and boy did she look good. Round two had finished at about 7:30pm and my dad still was not home.

"Denise, get dinner started while I go get your father, I won't be long."

Check this out Evangelist Millie Ann was on her way to the bar. She had on a black silk wrap around dress that clung to her curves and stopped right below the knees. The shoes matched to the T, and then she set it off with fat tennis bracelet. You couldn't miss the diamond crucifix that hung from her neck, it had just as many diamonds as the bracelet, and she looked hot!

Don't plant anything in your head, my mom had never smoked a cigarette or drank any hard liquor in her life. She would tell you in a minute, I belong to the Church of God in Christ and we practice holiness, not just by words but in our walk, hallelujah!

The funny part is that when she walked out the door I could see the lap cloth that she took to church with her hanging out the side of her purse, you know the one you put over your lap when your dress is too short. I love my momma she is always prepared.

It took a couple of weeks for me to get the nerve up to ask her what happened at the bar. She said that when she walked into the bar everyone just seemed to be staring at her. She wasn't sure if it was because she looked cute or because she was the oddball, anyway I know for myself she stuck out like a sore thumb. Trust me when I say the bar my dad hung out at had a reputation for harboring every type of criminal you could think of. Nevertheless she walked right in and sat next to my daddy. That's when the bartender walked over to her and said, "Long time no see Millie Ann what can I get for you?" she asked for a virgin Margarita. I almost fell out when she told me that, see momma was trying to be fast.

A couple of people walked over to tell her how much they missed her in praise and worship. She said that this really upset daddy. I think he felt like mom had come to blow up his spot. Ding, ding this was round three.

She said she told him how much she loved him and that she needed him to come home because she couldn't function anymore. Now I knew what, "no more" meant. Then she dropped the bomb on him. "If you are not home within the hour I will be packing your stuff."

There was no conversation after that because mom walked out. I tell you mom was a gangster for that one, because like I told you a while ago my dad was no punk. My daddy was king in his environment the same way my mom dominated her environment around church folks, so to save face he shouted, "don't bring yourself in here no more Millie!" I guess he had to save face some kind of way.

I tell you what daddy was home fifteen minutes after mom was. Daddy walked right in and slammed the door so hard that it don't hang right today.

"Don't ever come and fetch me like I'm a child, Millie Ann." He shouted, but momma was ready, she told him that his time was running short, and that he needed to make some decisions or someone would be leaving and it wouldn't be her.

"Either you're in or you're out what's it going to be?" Momma said.

I had finished cooking dinner, we sat together but there was no conversation. By now I knew my daddy wasn't going anywhere. I could also tell by the look on his face that he was shamed because he had treated mom so badly. But humility was not one of his strong points. Daddy got up from the table and went to go sit in his favorite chair.

"Grab me a beer, Denise." Daddy said.

"Not tonight Henry. I need your attention." Momma said. "We need to go upstairs and talk. We have a covenant relationship. You are my husband and I am your wife. You were raised in the church, that's where we met. The word of God says, "Train a child in the way he should go and he will not depart from it." If you have any love for me, and trust that the Lord will repair our relationship, come and talk with me."

As daddy walked up the stairs mom touched his back. Millie Ann was laying hands, passing on that same anointing and healing that had been passed on to her earlier through Mother Taylor.

I slept really well that night. I woke up to the smell of pancakes and sausage. I was so excited that I threw on my robe and went downstairs; daddy was sitting at the table eating.

"Good morning, baby girl, did you sleep well?"

Before I could answer, he was standing behind mom kissing her neck. You should have seen the smile on her face.

I thought about it and she didn't know how much of the truth she was stating. You see if it had not been for that incident with Nate their marriage would have never been restored.

"All things do come together for the good of those who know Him who have been called according to his purpose."

Hallelujah!!!